AF255887

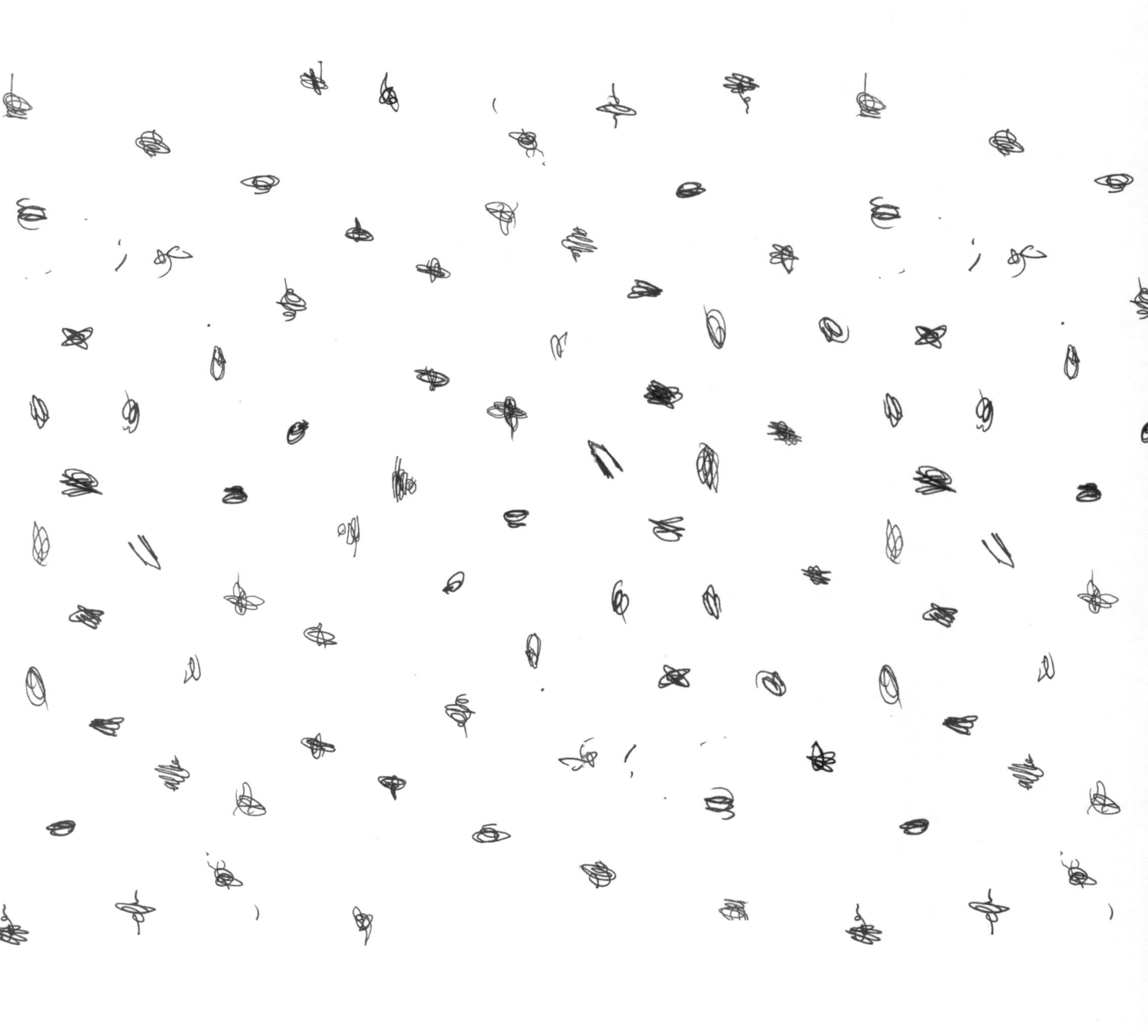

Publisher's Cataloging-in-Publication Data

Claud, Moriah
    Socks, cicadas, & other frustrations/
written by Moriah Claud/illustrated by Anna Thompson/pho-
tographs by Mikaela Hamilton
    ISBN 978-0-9882061-1-3

1. Poetry - General 2. Art: Techniques - Drawing 3. Art:
Individual Artists - General I. Title

Library of Congress Control Number: 2015954366

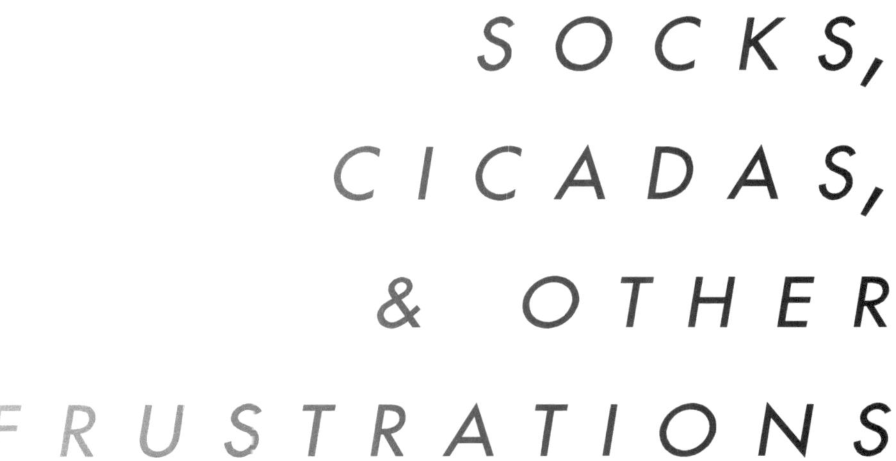

SOCKS, CICADAS, & OTHER FRUSTRATIONS

written by Moriah Claud
illustrations by Anna Thompson
photographs by Mikaela Hamilton

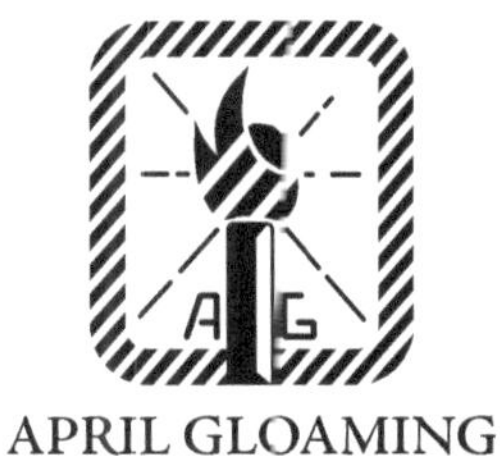

APRIL GLOAMING

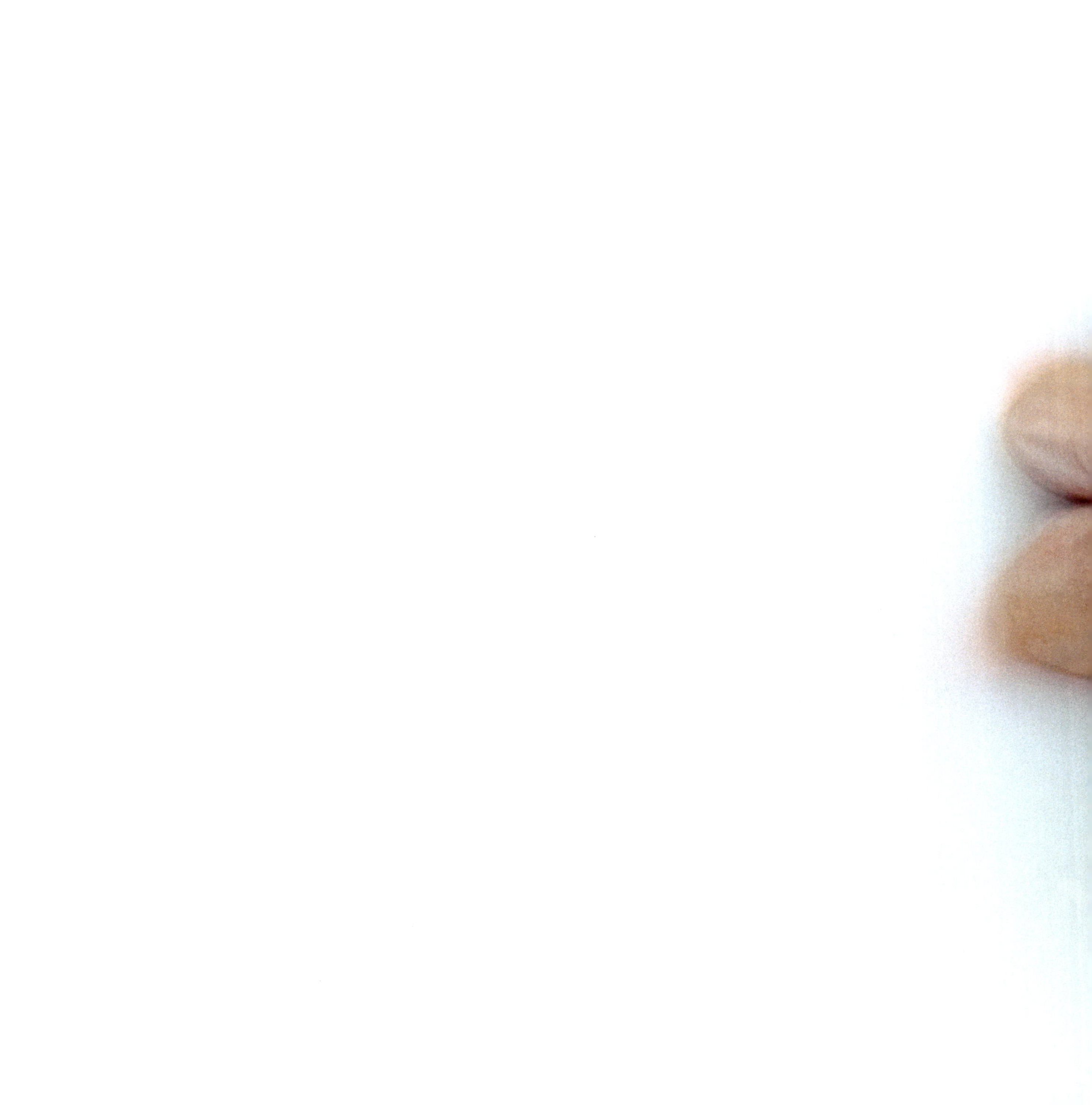

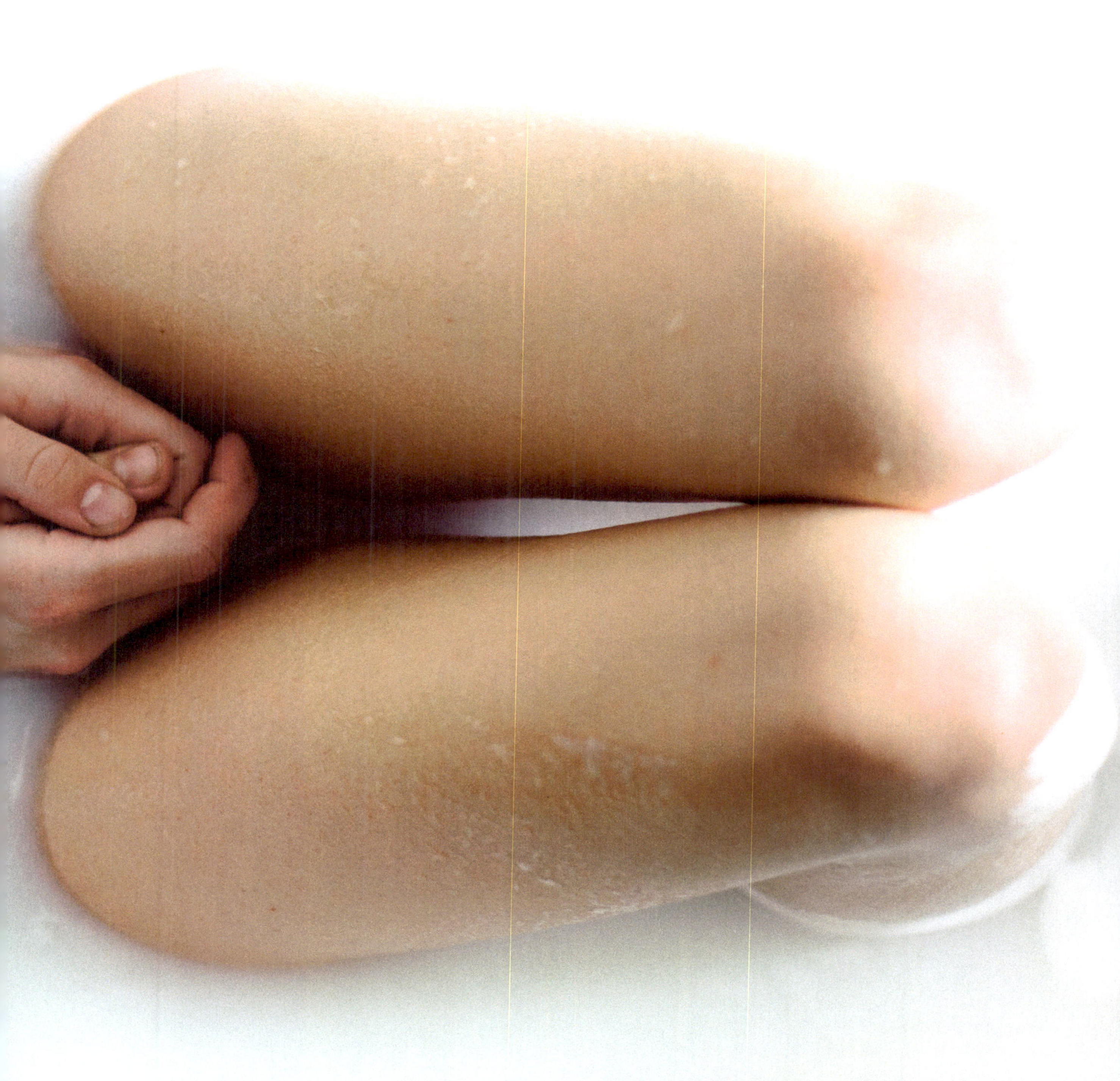

MIKAELA [*PHOTOGRAPHY*]

Mikaela Hamilton is a travel + portrait photographer based in Nashville, TN. Born with a bout of wanderlust, she spends most of her free time traveling and eating tacos. She is passionate about community and creative collaboration and considers it an honor to work alongside such talented, badass women.

ANNA [*BOOK DESIGN / ILLUSTRATION*]

Anna Thompson is a book designer, illustrator, and printmaker based in New York City. Before moving to the city to work in publishing, Anna lived in the Hudson valley at the Women's Studio Workshop, a printmaking studio that publishes handmade artist books. There, she enjoyed rural life and helped run the papermaking, letterpress, etching, and silkscreen studios.

MORIAH [*POETRY*]

Moriah Claud is a writer living in Nashville, TN where she recently received her B.A. in English from Lipscomb University. Like most writers and former English majors, Moriah is also a barista and a server. Her great passions include: coffee, stories, IPAs, and the appropriate use of the possessive pronoun "your."

Socks, Cicadas, & Other Frustrations is a collaborative project using poetry, photography, and illustrations to tell a story from three unique perspectives. The book attempts to offer an interpretation of the experience of art by offering visual representations of each poem.

It seems equally relevant to briefly describe what the book is about. As the poet and the subject of the photographs, this book is about standing naked in the middle of a freeway singing a song you thought was Adele in the wrong key. Broadly, it's about everything that scares me. The book describes growing up, learning to understand pain, and accepting who you are outside of who you thought you'd be. More specifically, Socks, Cicadas, & Other Frustrations is about three artists trying to capture the vulnerability of loving oneself.

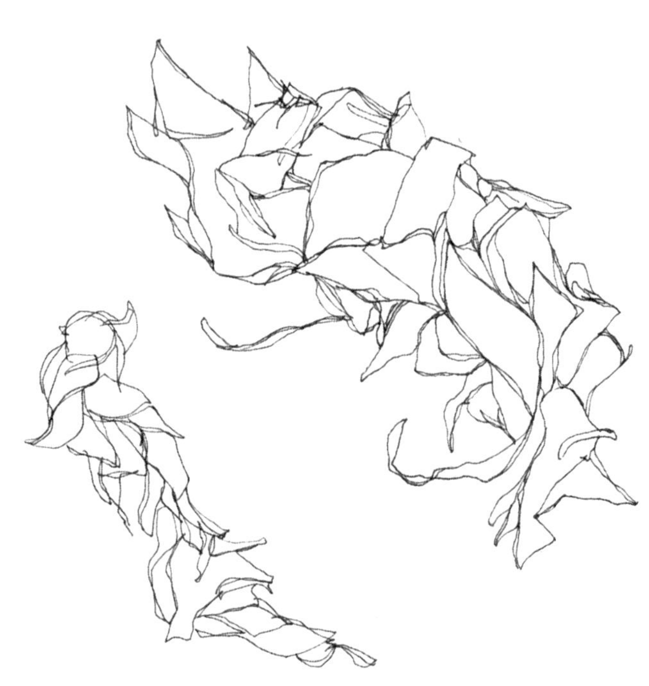

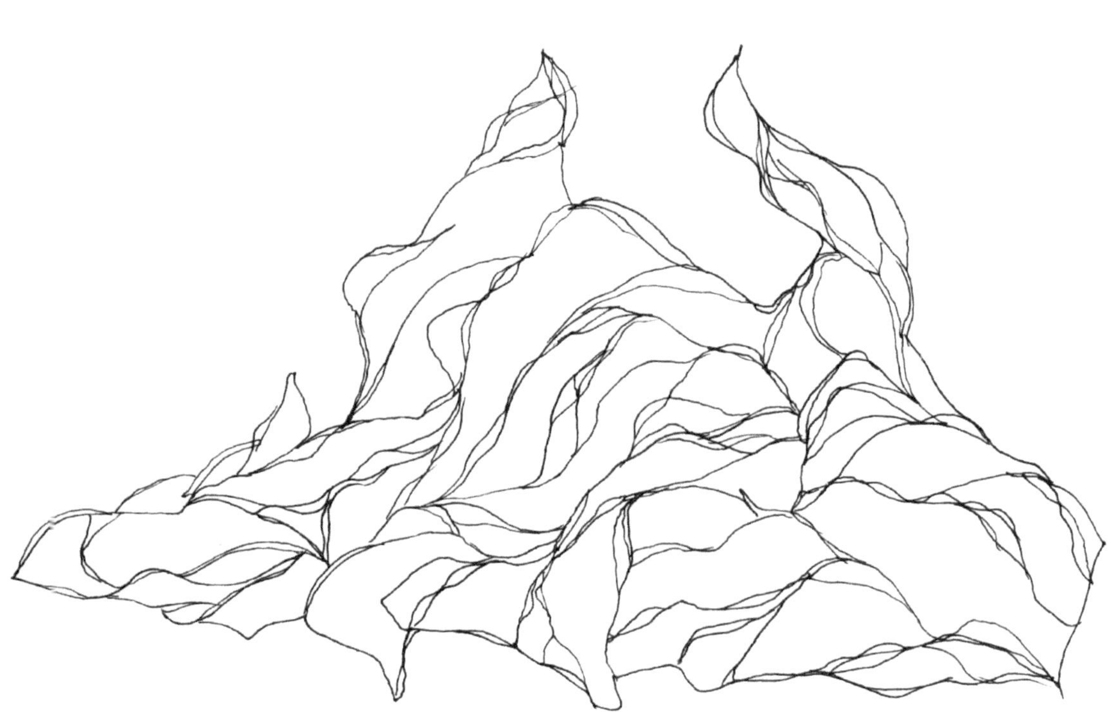

SOCKS

Some day you will wake to find yourself lying in the middle of your father's empty home and when you do, don't run. When you run, you will find that everything you knew about running was wrong and you'll forget which arm should swing with which leg. There's a rhythm to it, don't forget. Once you've forgotten how to run, you will stop moving. Even your eyelashes will stop moving. Only your chest keeps rising and falling. When you look at your hands, you will notice they're shaking and your feet are cold, but don't sit down. If you sit down, you'll fall asleep in your father's empty home.

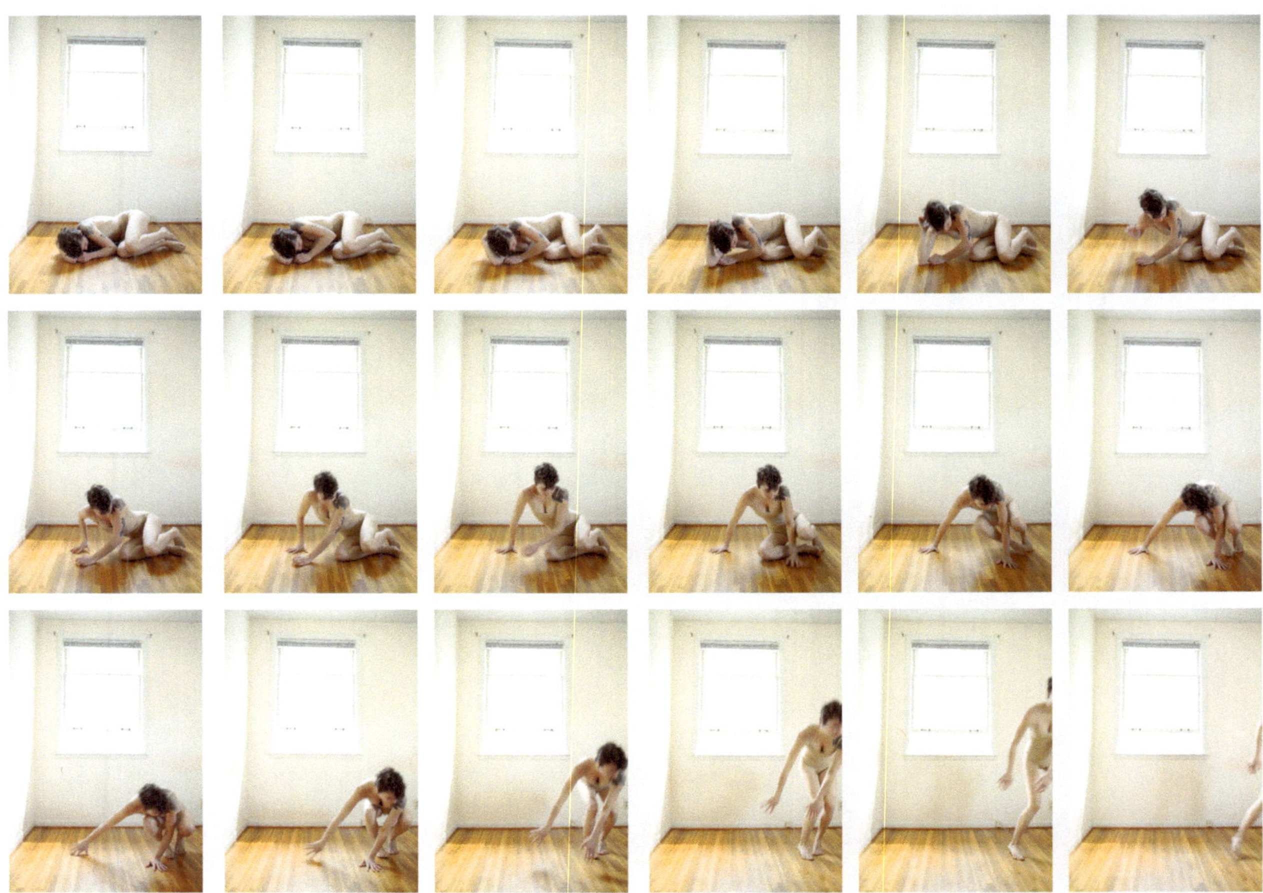

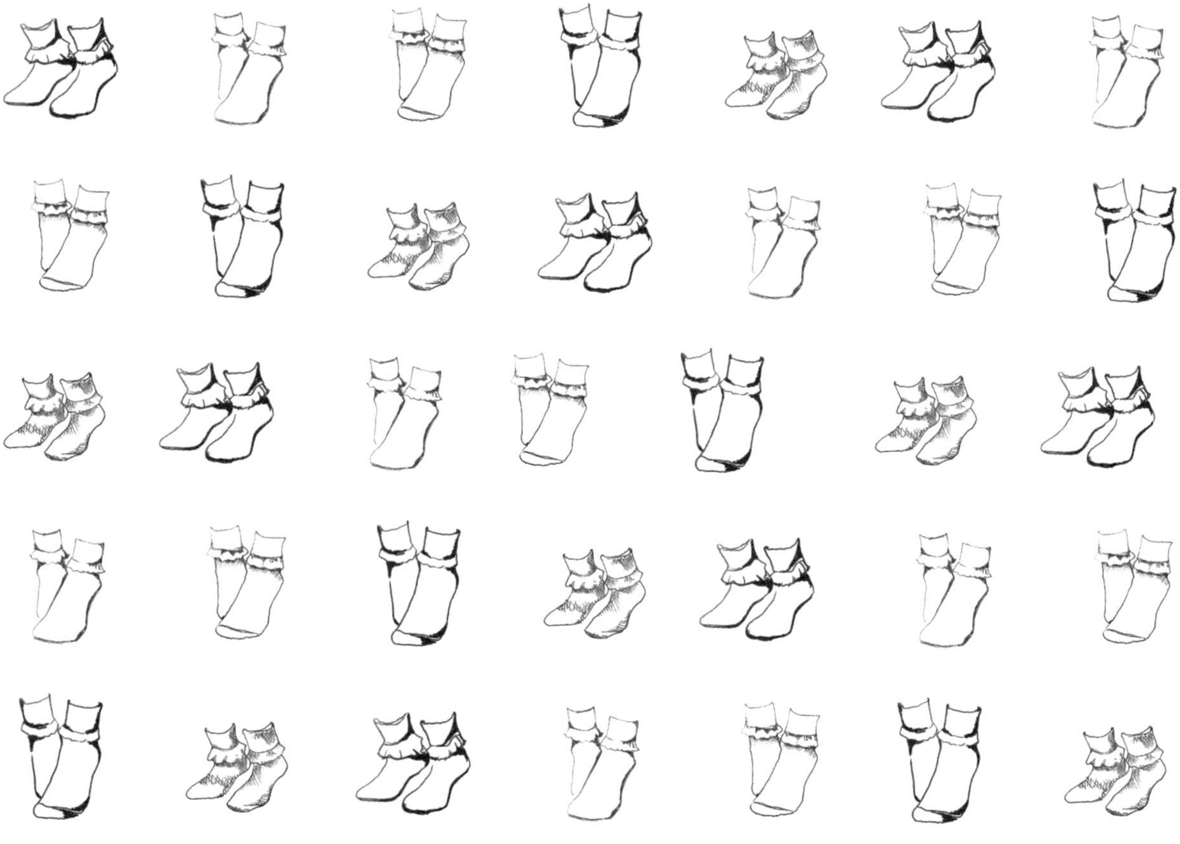

I was taught to be a certain kind of person, a piece to fit in a place, but I'm not the missionary or the mother or the little girl with lacy socks sitting quietly in the second row.

I ran away, losing pieces between cushions or thrown out with empty bottles until I couldn't tell which way was forward or which socks were mine.

Isn't it a shame to find me here, far from my place in the second pew, missing so many pieces? Some days I miss the quiet place you planned for me, but somewhere I lost the lace from my socks and I'm a lot of things I wasn't supposed to be.

For years we
hid our freckles
with prayers,
and made our-
(perfect) selves
in mirrors.

Our entire lives
we heard
what it means
to be broken
and thought
we looked
(so convincingly)
held together.

We arranged our-
selves to look
(somewhat)
right, but my
eyebrows
always grew
too close and
your nose was
always broken.

So we tried
covering our-
selves in
blue cloth to
match the walls
where we whispered
the same prayers
as our fathers.

You didn't believe
my eyes
(blue-green
like my father's)
when I said
you shouldn't need
forgiveness.

You said
(so confidently)
that we could
only become
ourselves.

We'll return,
years from now,
without a prayer
for the bright-
stained windows
whose blue light will
trace the angles
of your nose
and bring out
my freckles.

We're not holy
anymore
(we never were,
really).

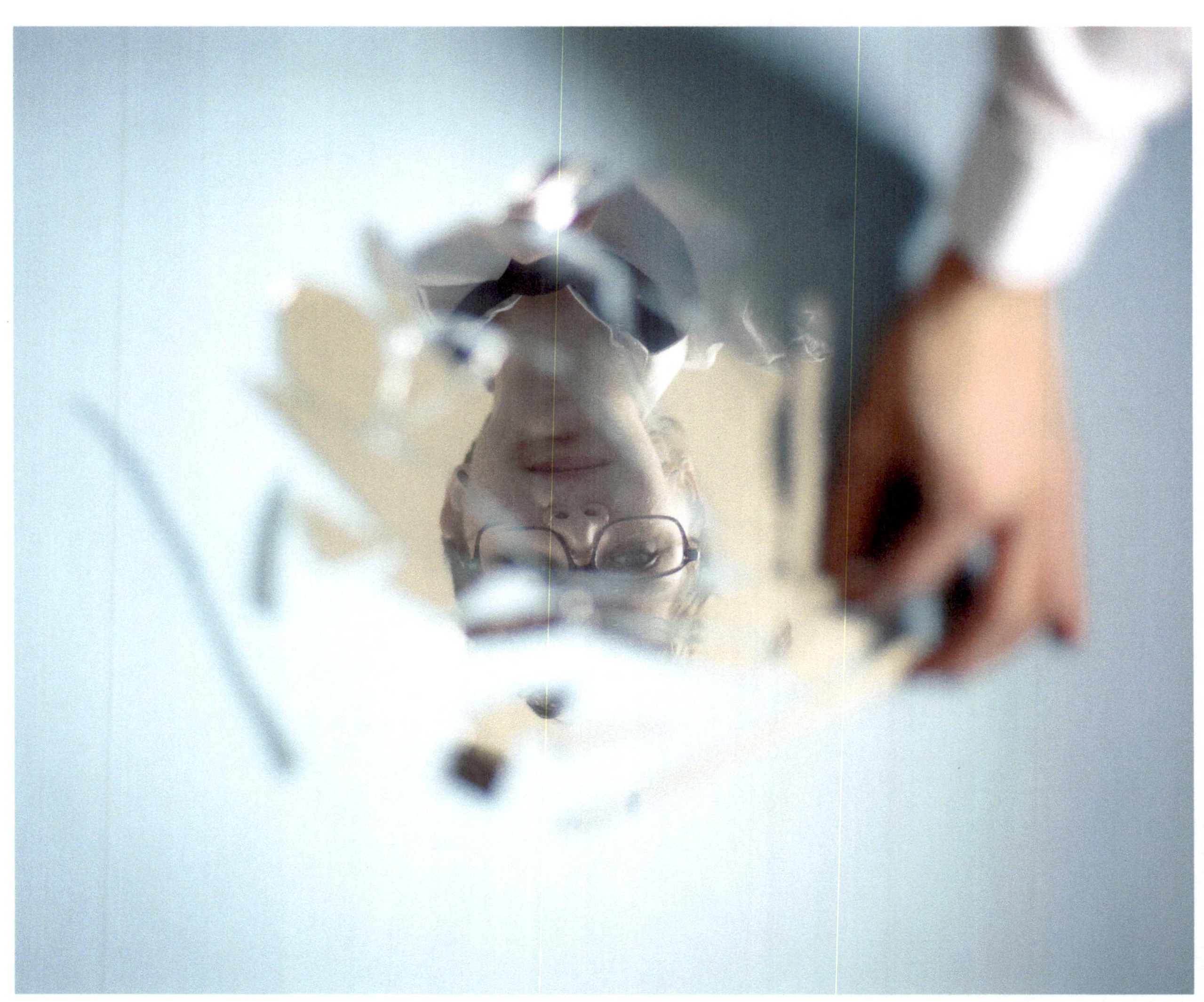

When we were small
we played games like hide and seek.
We'd close our eyes and count loudly
and I always hid in the same places.
I never liked the waiting once I heard the
here I come,
and when the cabinet doors flew open
we would scream
and I would run.

We're too big for games now
but I never stopped playing hide and seek.
I'm always hiding in the same places
but there's no one counting
and no one shouts
ready or not
so I know to be
quiet and
still and
hide.

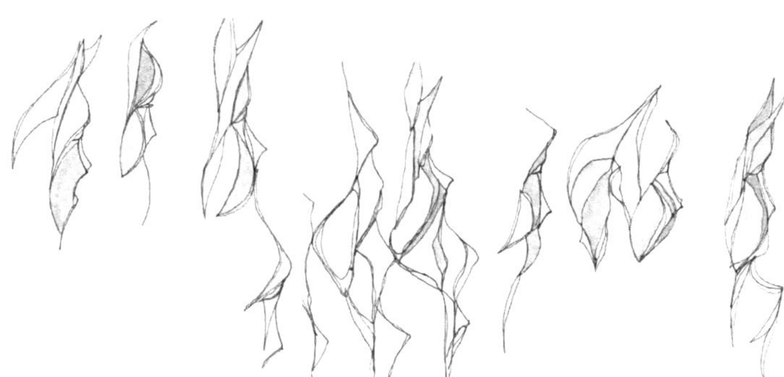

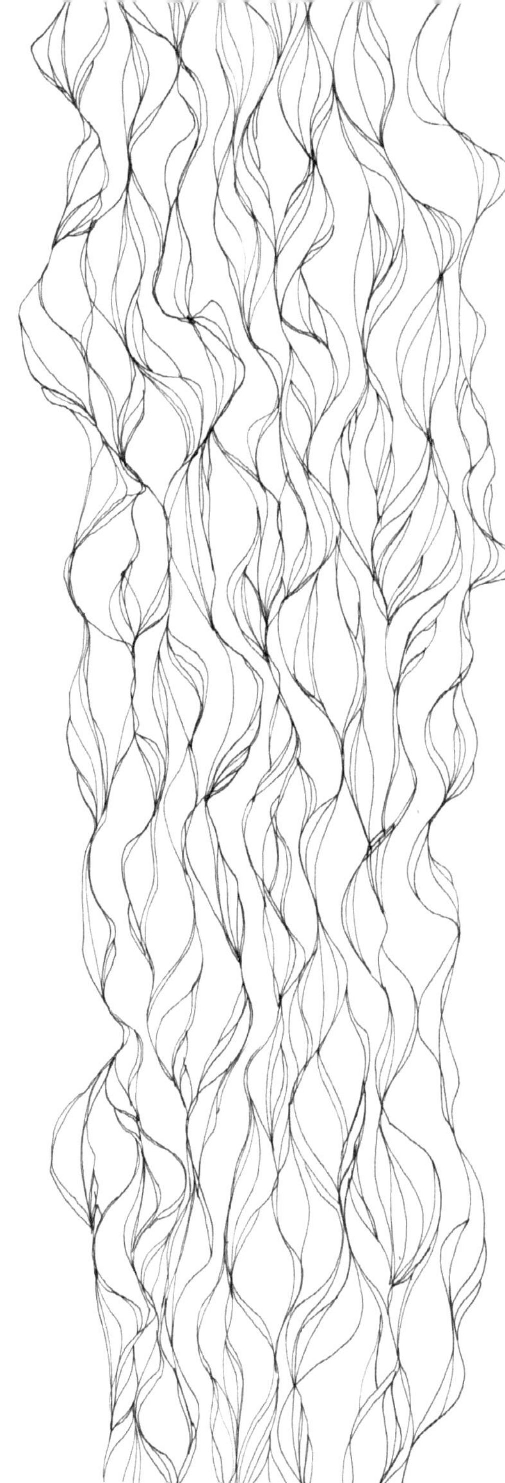

When you were made, you took your father's eyes and your mother's hands. You took other things too. Even your name came from someone else, and no one made your eyelashes or the shape of your fingernails. You will spend most of your life looking for the rest of your body. Some day you will look at the veins in your hands and the veins in the leaves of a willow tree, and you will realize you were made from borrowed things and you know nothing about creation.

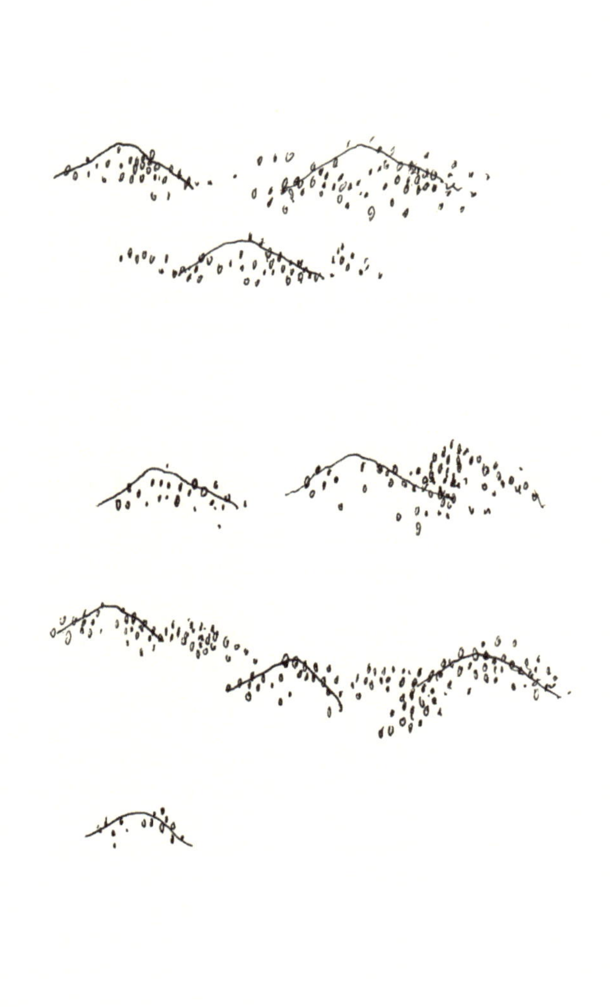

CICADAS

I was beautiful
once,
for a summer,
and I would stare at my reflection
and think about the eyes
that tore through my clothes
and never looked at my face,
and I learned to believe that my body was cruel
and my lips were cruel and I had no one to blame
but myself.

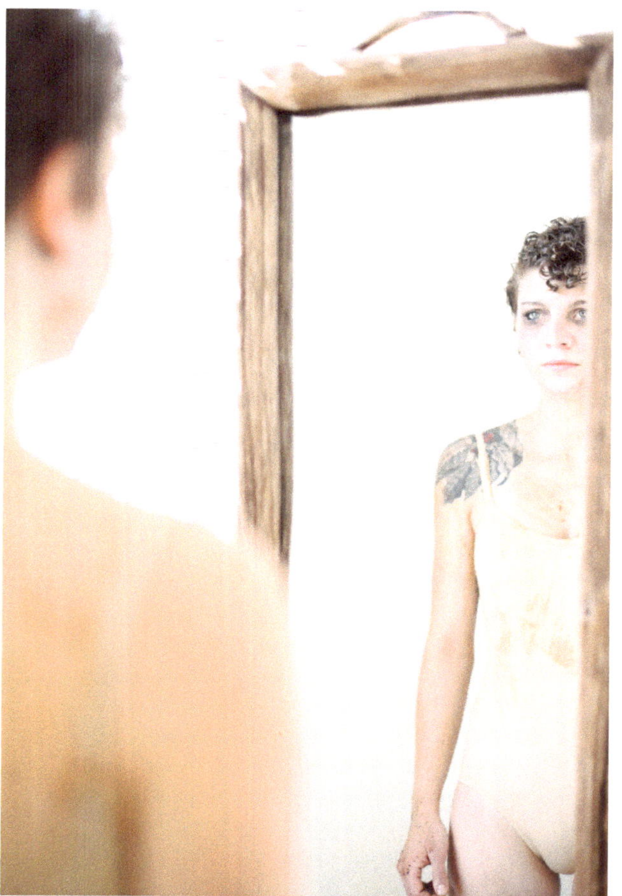

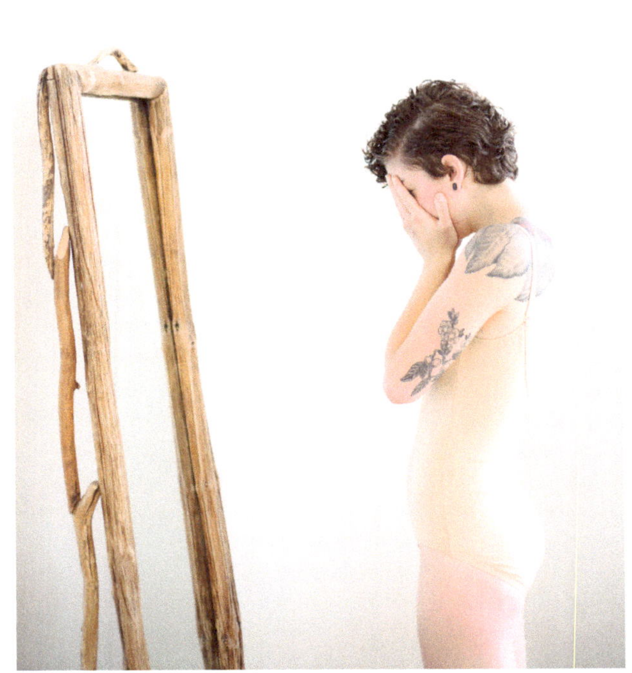

So when you asked me if
I feel beautiful,
holding my face in your hands,
I couldn't look in your eyes
because I am cruel
so I closed my eyes and tried not to see
my dirty reflection
or remember the way hands make me hollow
so I just touched my cruel lips
between your blue eyes
and I didn't answer.

We would find them squished
in door frames and plastered
across windshields.

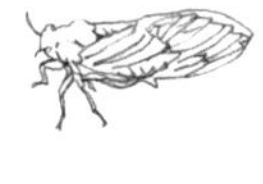

At night, the sound
of their screeching wings
could muffle a car accident.
Did muffle a car accident$_1$.

*1. An unfortunate incident that happens unintentionally
and unexpectedly, usually resulting in damage or injury.
In this case, accident refers less to the unintentional
but to the unexpected nature of the incident
and the damage resulting therein.*

For further information, see also victim.

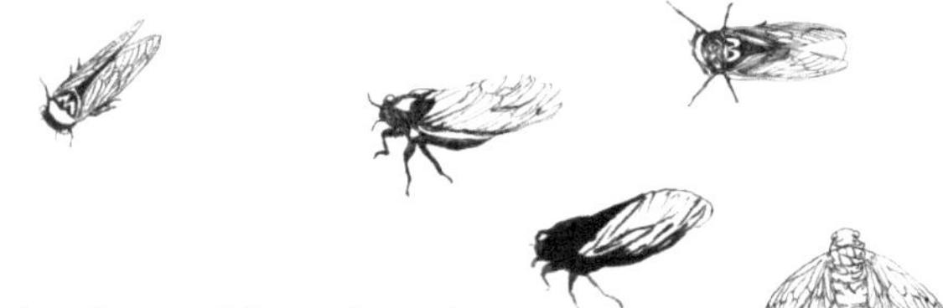

On the day the world would end:

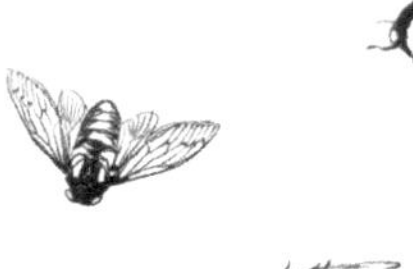
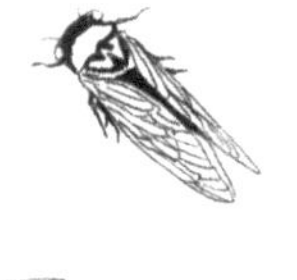
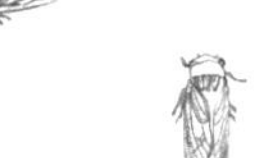

The Mayans said the
world would end
the same day I heard
you had created life.

Maybe the world will end
before you can tell
your daughters you are
sorry for the things you
did or before you see
in her the girls you
named hateful things2.

2. We are all asking for it, after all,
with our lips and our legs and the way
we smoke cigarettes on the back porch.*

** See also deserve.*

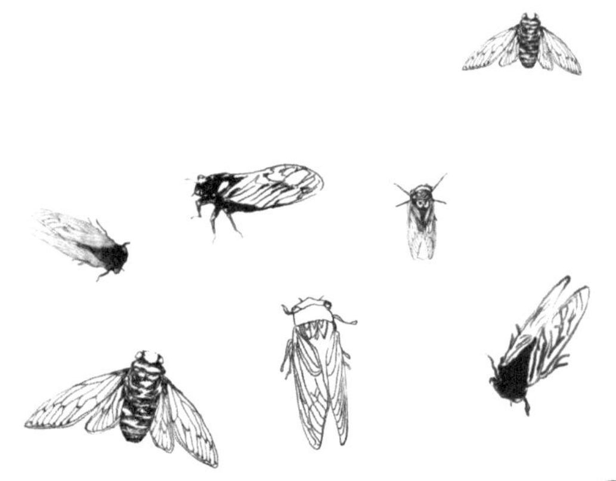

In the month of pi:

Everything depends on numbers
and the circumference of a circle$_3$
depends on the length of the radius
and no matter where you stand on
the edge you can't determine which
way is forward or backward
or how far you stand
from the other side.

In the middle of the 3rd month
I found myself standing where
I've stood 3.14 times before—
when everything I knew
about probability was lost.

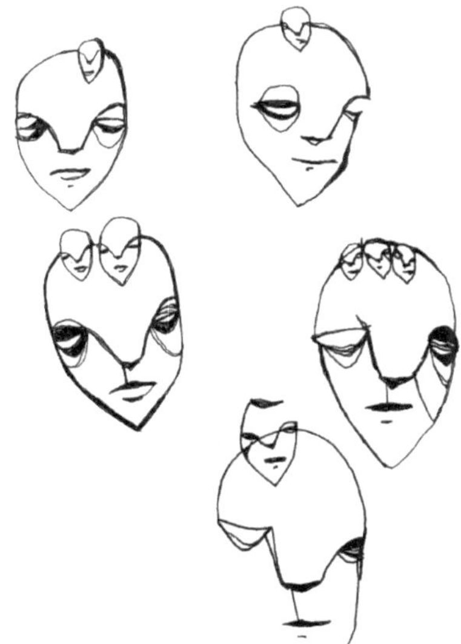

3. Circle: the constant illusion of a change in direction.*
(3.14159265358979328462643383279502884197...)

**See also sadness.*

I like it here – curled together
like cursive letters bending
to form words that ask

permission. Your skin sticks
where our ribs make brackets
around sentences we haven't

quite read. I should be afraid
of your eyes and your arms
or maybe that my own hands

will deflate my ribs like a
crushed balloon and show
you what's between my

sternum and spine.

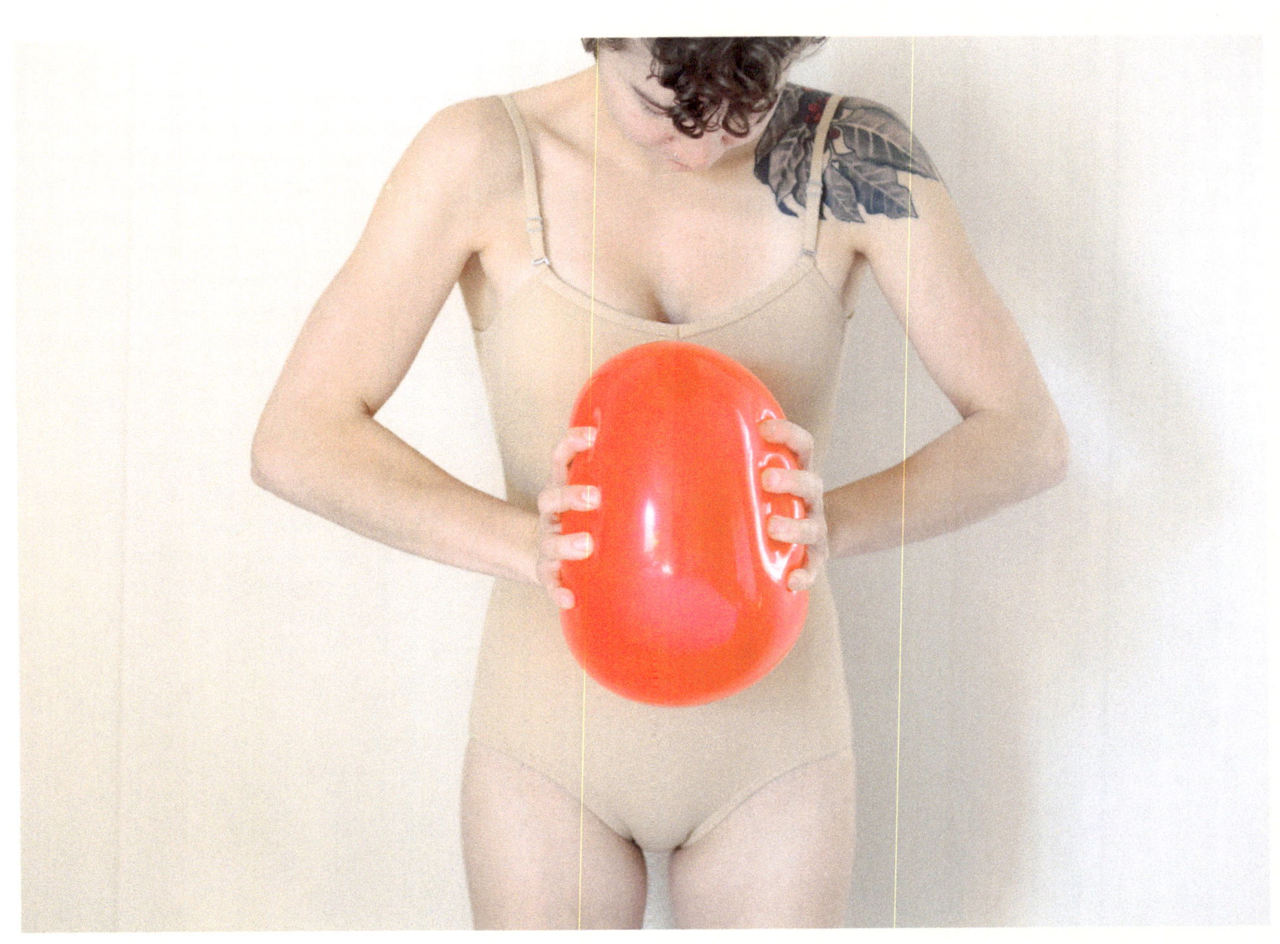

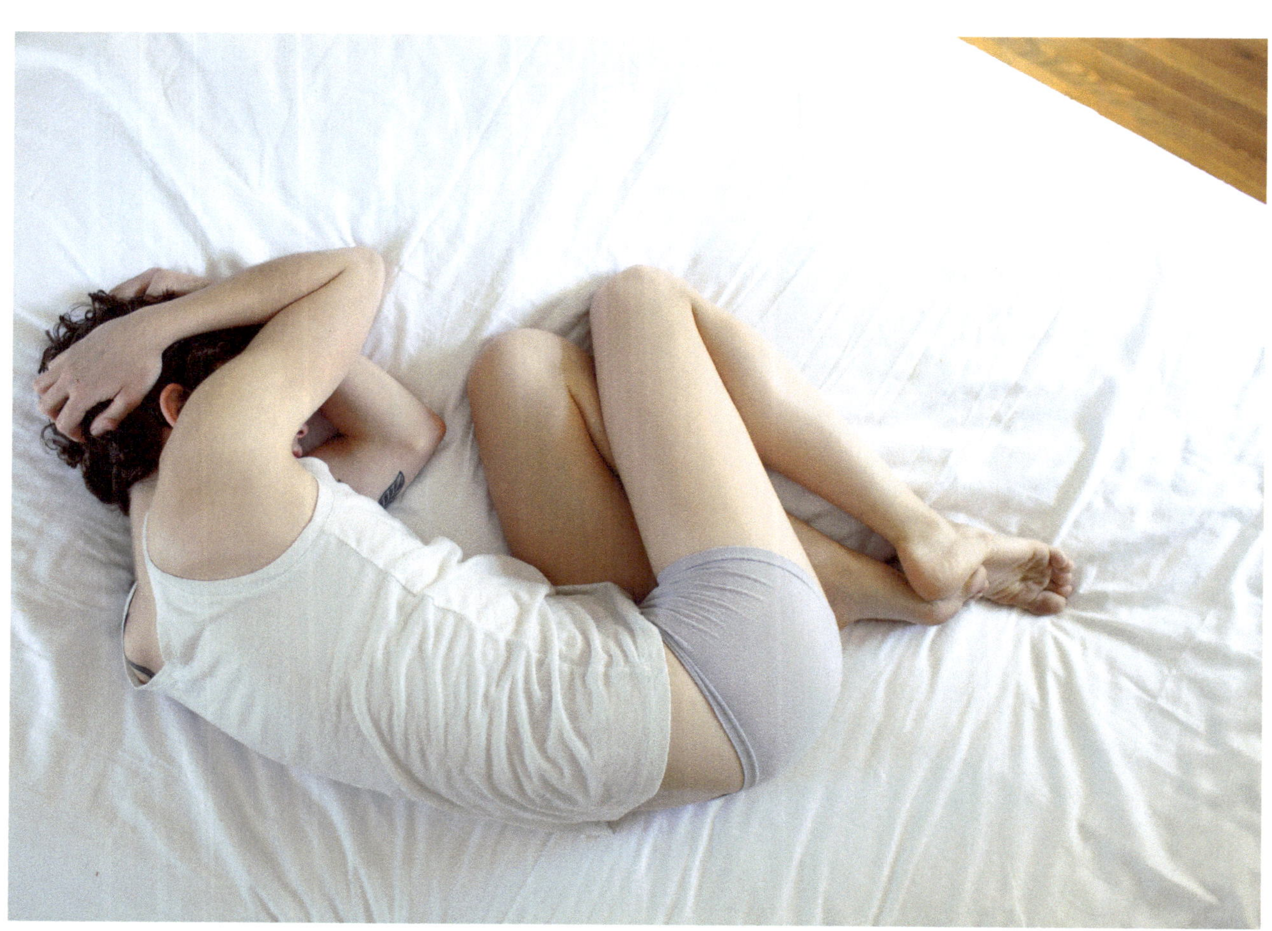

and God has many other surprises, like
when you woke up from your dream and realized
there was no Henry, only John and was that okay?

Will He surprise me too, like
when I fall asleep next to him and
feel his warm breath against
my neck, will I dream about
the man I fear the most?
I hope I dream of Henry and I hope that's okay.

Or will I wake to find them
both gone, like a prayer
left half-answered and will I be okay?

There is a Henry, John. I'm sorry that I said that.

When you get tired of running and sleeping you will lose your arms and feet and hands, but don't be afraid. Once you've lost your legs, you will have only one rib you borrowed from a stranger. You will break your borrowed rib and be re-membered. Your legs will be replaced with new ones that swing awkwardly with your new arms and feel your new chest will rise and fall. You will work so hard to be re-membered, but your hands will always shake and when your new feet get cold you will sit down. You will find the rest of your body when you stop sleeping in empty houses.

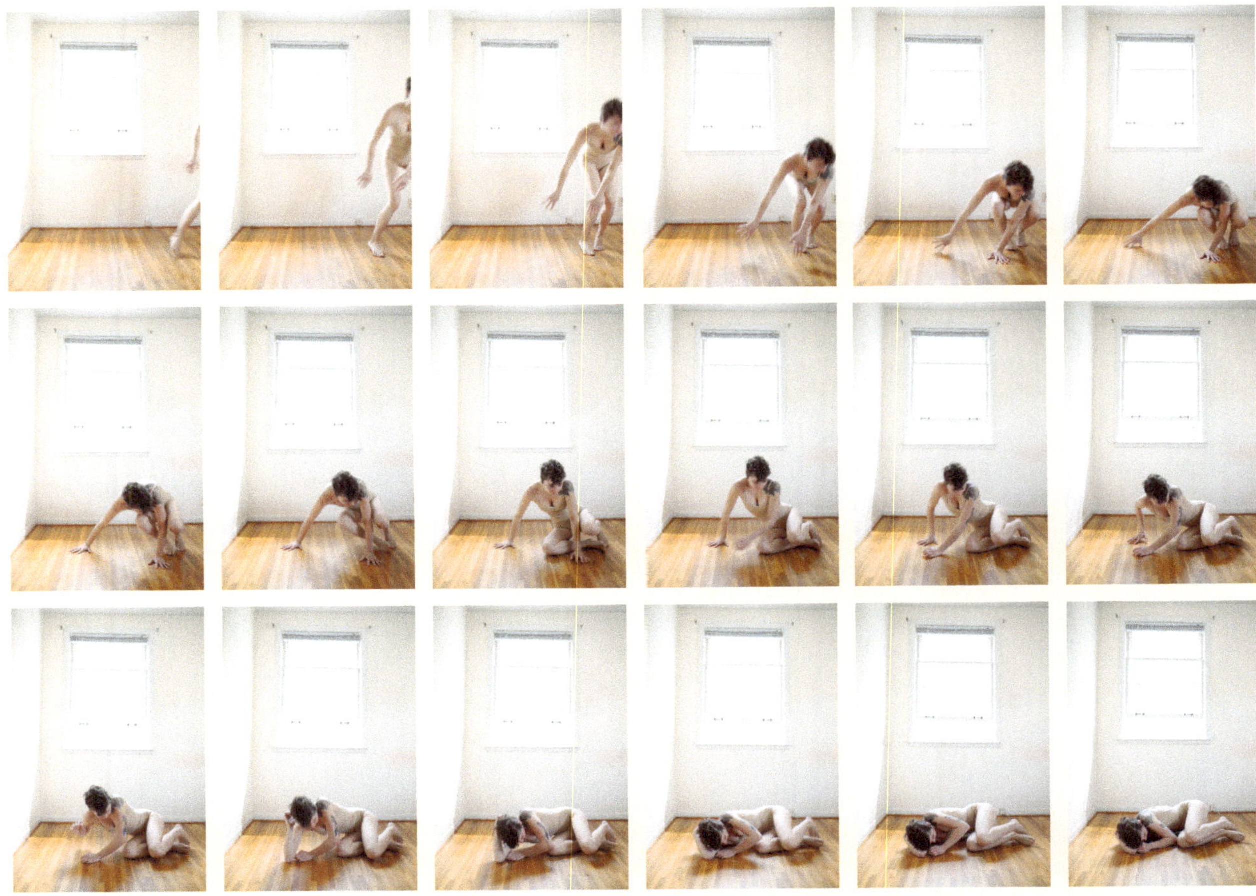

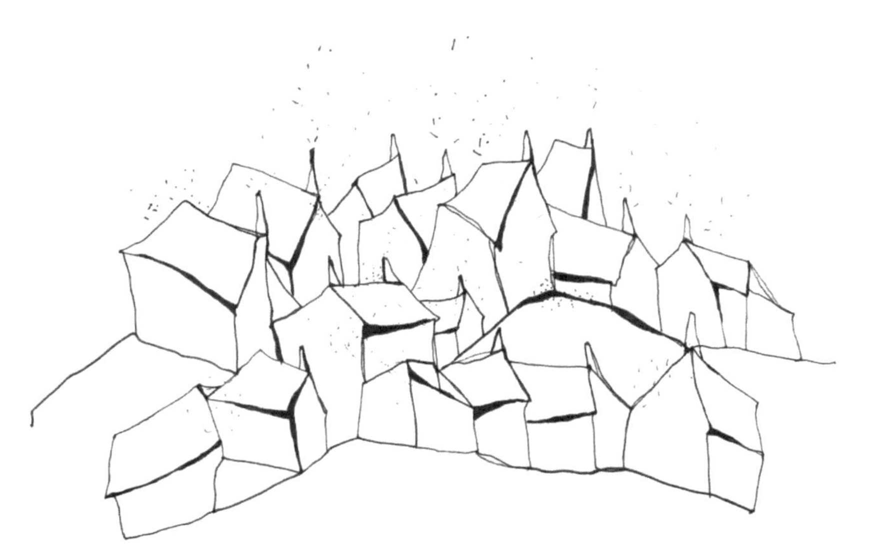

OTHER

FRUSTRATIONS

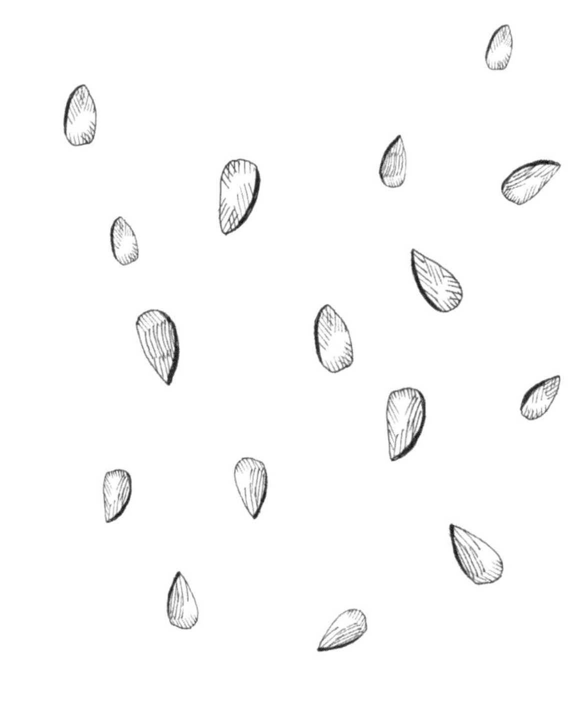

"The scent of bitter almonds
would always remind him
of the fate
of unrequited love."
— Gabriel Garcia Marquez,
Love in the Time of Cholera

The hardest part of the
fear of feeling wanted
is that I want only what
doesn't want me back.

The hardest part of my
addiction to almonds
is the unrelenting
want to feel wanted.

If I locked a thousand words in a box
    and called them poetry
    and told you they were   beautiful
would you want them

    I deposit them on slips of paper—
    my useless skill—
hoping to save enough to be valuable
and when I throw my box into a pool
    of dead water
    I will drown with them

    when my box of words and I
    are dragged from the bottom of
    the dead pool
        will anyone be saved?

the valiant will spread us out to dry
and we will become porcelain and   beautiful—
    immobile as art

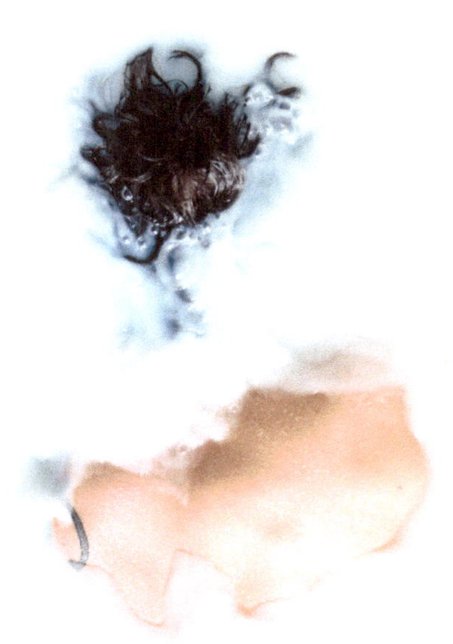
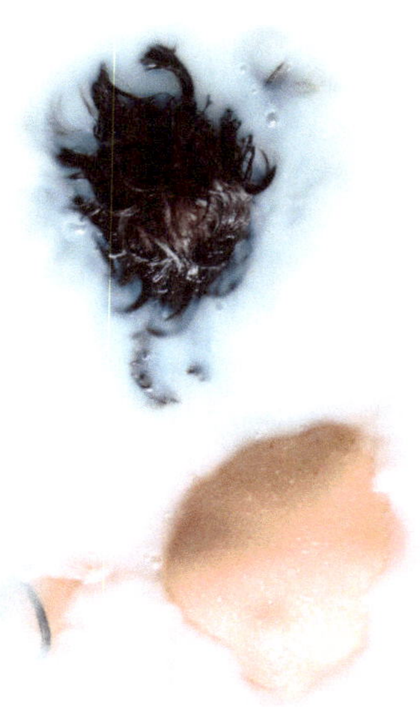

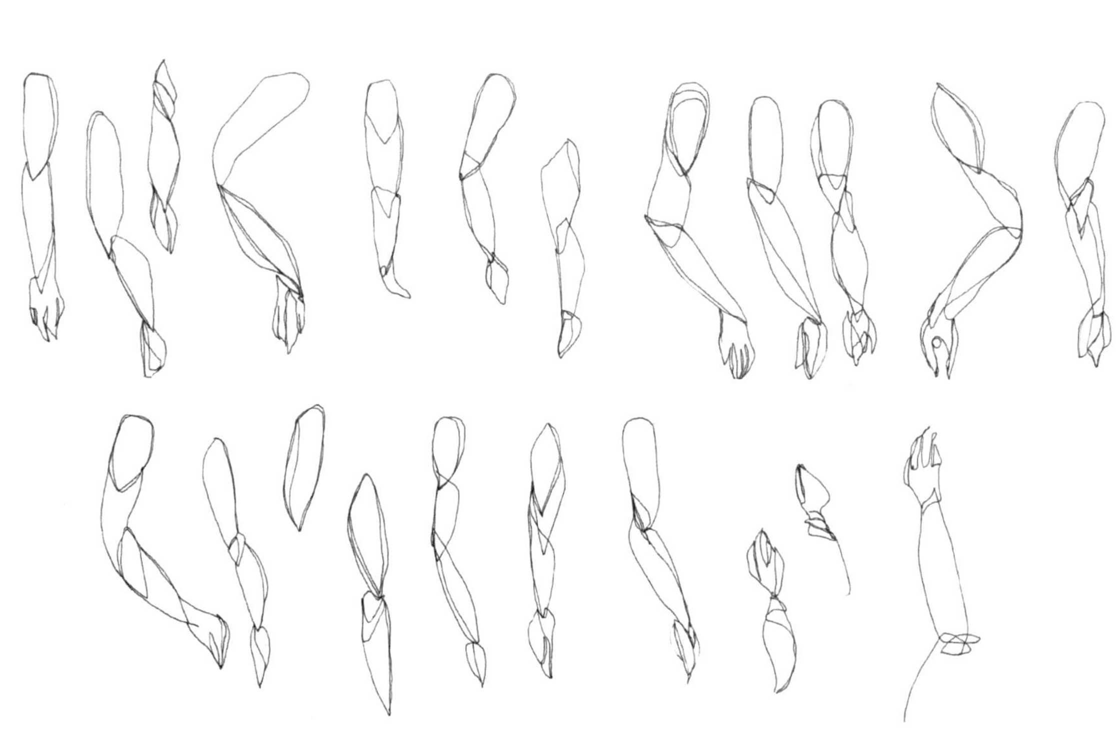

I wake up
with an arm wrapped gently
over your side
and for a moment I forget
that you don't want me.
I lie there,
holding the warmth of your body
close to mine
until the moment passes
and I remember that
holding you is just a dream,
and I think about
touching my lips
to the back of your neck
as a quiet consolation,
but I know that touching
my lips to your neck
won't wake me up
and when you stir
and turn your sleepy
eyes to mine,
I smile and roll away
and try my best
to stop dreaming.

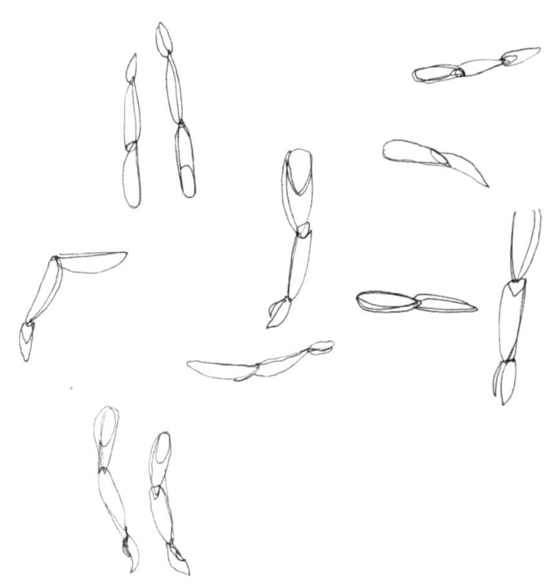

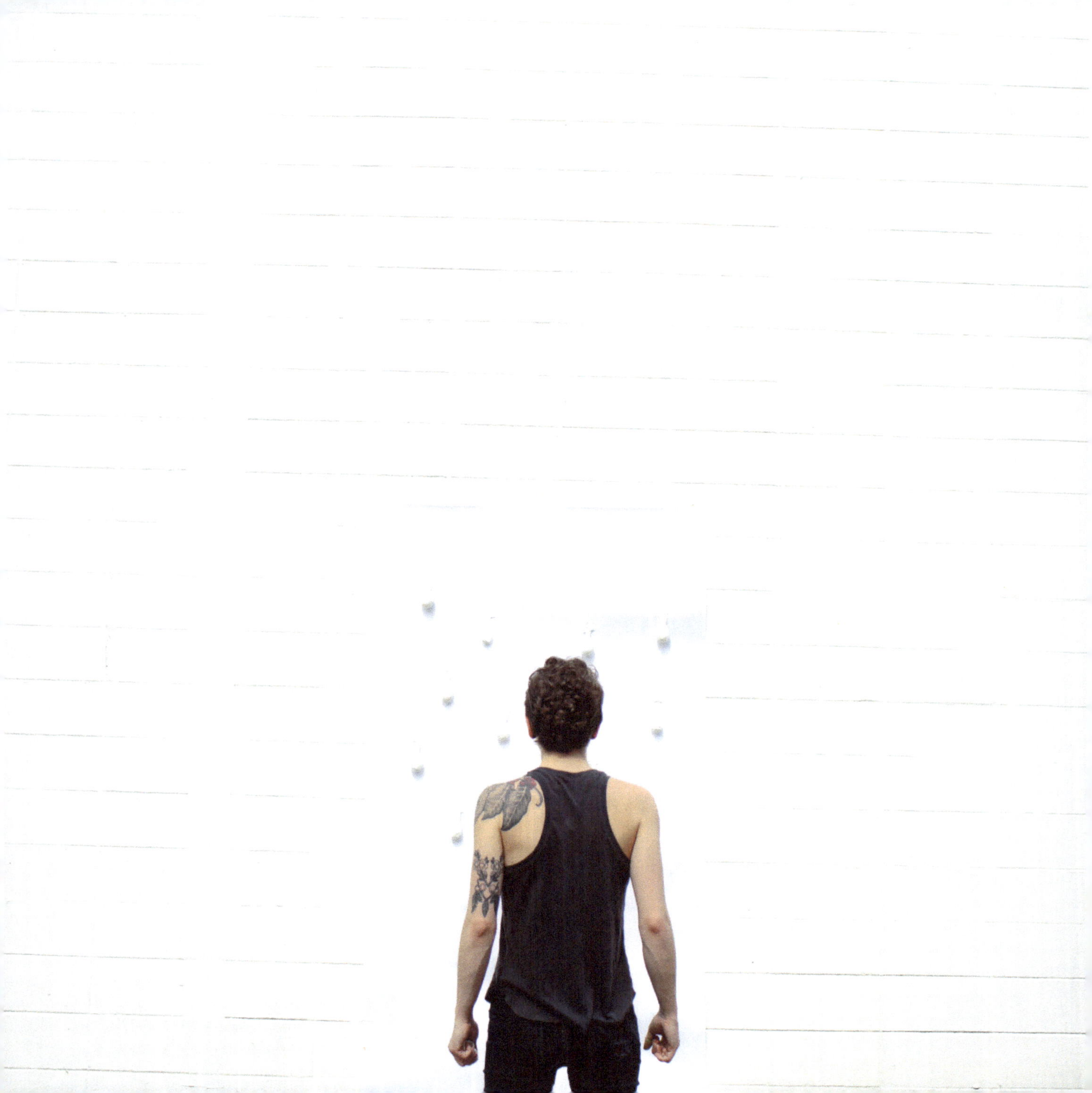

{the difference between *identity* and *identification* is more than a suffix}

Webster defines identity as *who someone is* or
the distinguishing character or personality of an individual.

Identity is a noun.

Webster defines identification as *the act of finding out who someone
is or the act of identifying someone.*

Identification is also a noun.

identity

At 22 I fell in love with a tall, blonde man who held my face in his hands
and never made me afraid. Later that same week, I fell in love with a
brunette who told me to never stop creating. Her smile made my ears go
numb. This was very confusing.

identification

     I read a book that said sociopaths tend to be bisexual.
     My therapist told me that victims of sexual assault often question
     or change their sexual preference.

I don't think I'm a sociopath. Or a victim, most of the time.

     According to my driver's license, I am a 5'6" female with
     green eyes.

I decided that I would only ever fall in love with a close friend.
The next day I fell in love with a close friend.
Three days later, she told me she was broken.
        {I should have mentioned that I'd already stored my whole
        heart just behind the brown flecks in her eyes}

identification

Romantic: marked by an imaginative or emotional appeal to what is
heroic, remote, adventurous, or idealized. (See also: putting your heart
in the wind for love; the most beautiful human thing to do; a priceless act)

identity

Romantic: impractical in conception or plan; idealized; idealized;
idealized. (see also: storing one's whole heart just behind the color in
another's eye; considering that another may not want one's whole heart
but placing it there anyways; a devastating cycle)

identity
Sometimes
I've stored my
whole heart
behind the color
in so many eyes
I can see it beating
behind the
blue-brown-green
flecks in every
stranger's eye
I see.

identification

I don't mean to be so careless.

identity

I have learned that it is impractical for one to throw one's
whole heart into the wind when
     (a) there is no wind and
     (b) one is facing a wall.

identification

{I've been throwing things at the same
walls for so long that people have started
mistaking my poor aim for art.}

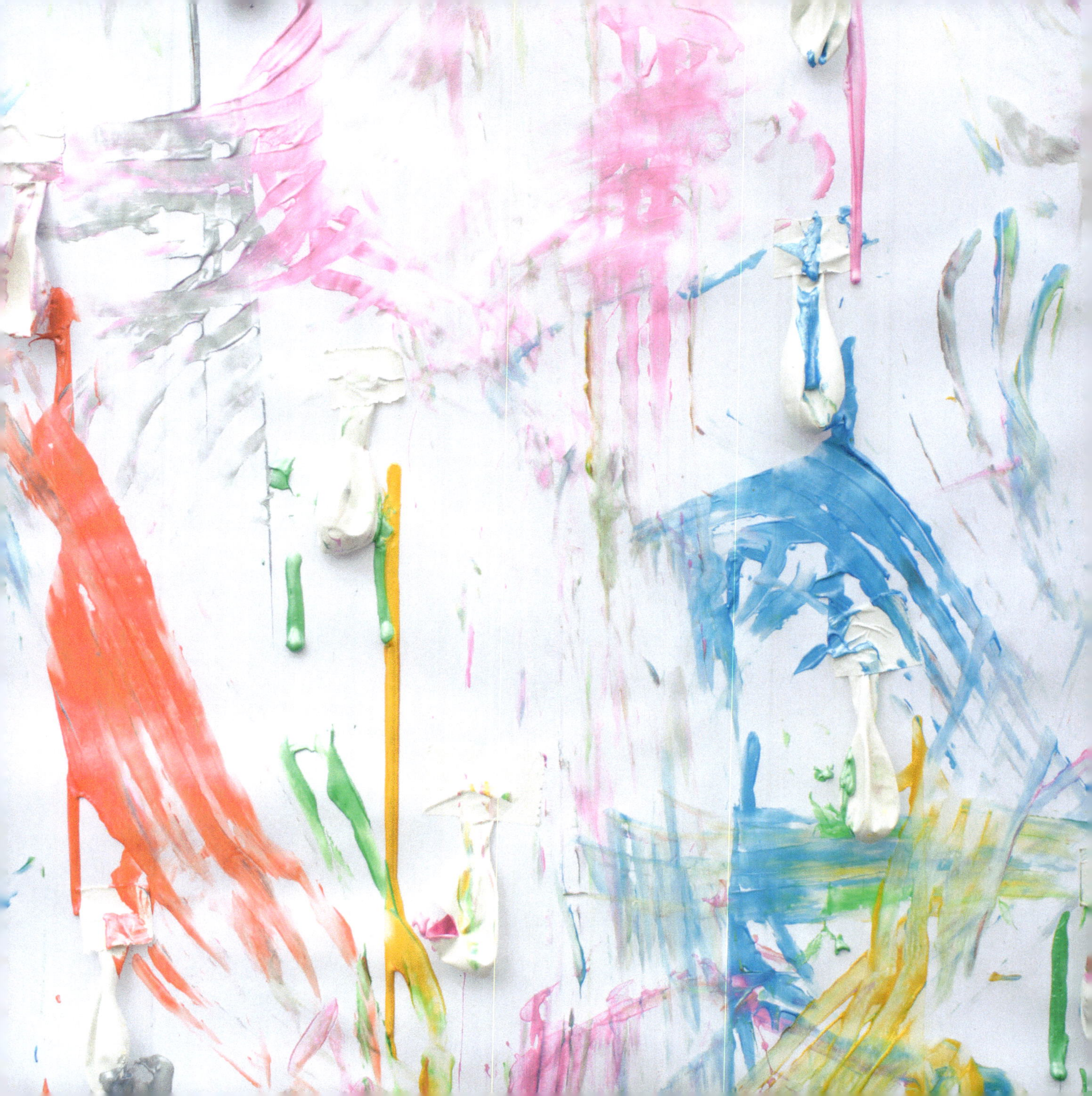

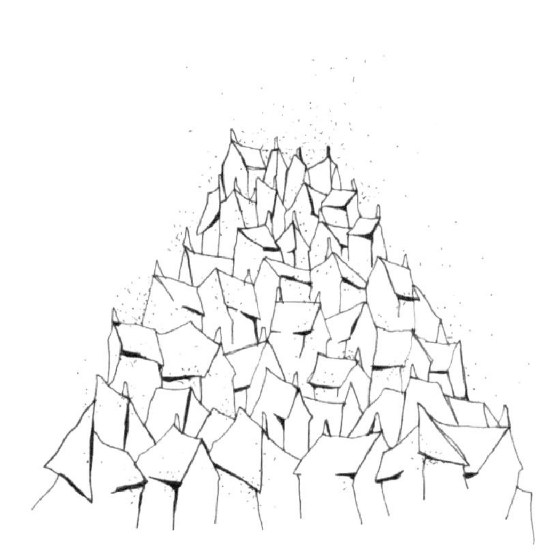

For a long time, you'll live on a line. One day, when you're still young, that line will splinter, and that splinter will splinter and all those fractures will scare you, and it will keep going until your whole life looks like a willow tree turned upside down. But one day you'll stand in the middle of your splintered willow and notice that it's still linear and you're still young and dumb but not so afraid.

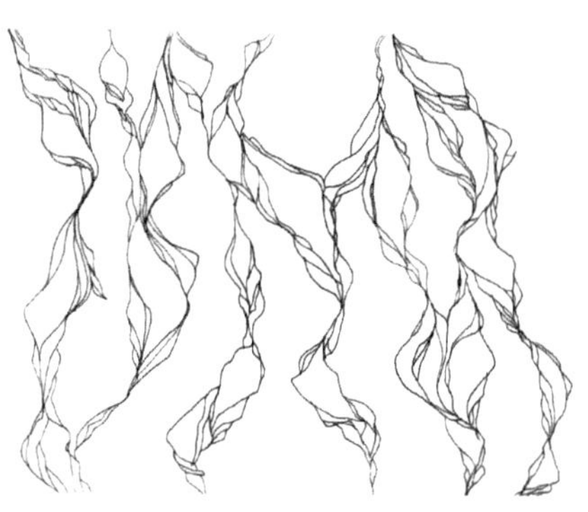

ACKNOWLEDGMENTS

I have more thanks to give than there is space on this page. First and foremost, I am unbelievably grateful to Anna and Mikaela for not only being willing to join me in this project, but for making it the beautiful work of art it is. I never would have had the courage to share this without you guys.

Thank you, Jan Harris, for everything you taught me and for believing in me more than I ever did. Thanks to my wives, Lexi Koczanski and Patrick Rush, for keeping me alive with wine and pizza and all the love a girl could ask for. Thank you Alex Claud and Shanley Deignan for always encouraging me to be myself (Tripod forever). Thanks to Reggie and Jackie Claud and my beautiful sisters for loving their "wild card" middle child unconditionally.

Thank you Georgia for letting me fill your bathtub with milk and not getting mad when I broke your French press. Thanks to the people at the random warehouse for letting a couple of strange young women throw paint at your wall. Thank you Lauren Hill for putting up with Mikaela and I breaking mirrors and bursting flour filled balloons in our home. Thank you beer. Thank you coffee. Thank you pizza. Thanks to Nick Rossi and Sobotka Literary Magazine for sharing my words. Thank you Robyn Leigh Lear and the Regenerates for making me a part of your community. Thanks to all of you who have followed this project through its seemingly endless process. Thank you Nashville for supporting creativity and being so extraordinarily weird.

Finally, thank you, reader.